THE
YALE SERIES OF YOUNGER POETS
EDITED BY STEPHEN VINCENT BENÉT

PERMIT ME VOYAGE

AMS PRESS
NEW YORK

PERMIT ME VOYAGE

BY JAMES AGEE

WITH A FOREWORD BY

ARCHIBALD MacLEISH

NEW HAVEN
YALE UNIVERSITY PRESS
1934

Copyright © 1934 by Yale University Press; renewed 1962
by the James Agee Trust

Reprinted by arrangement with Houghton Mifflin Company
First AMS EDITION published 1971
Manufactured in the United States of America

International Standard Book Number:
  Complete Set: 0-404-53800-2
  Volume 33: 0-404-53833-9

Library of Congress Card Catalog Number: 70-144740

AMS PRESS, INC.
NEW YORK, N.Y. 1(

PS
3501
.G35
P4
1934
811 Ag32p

Agee, James

Permit me voyage

Foreword.

THERE is an impression, diligently fostered by at least one literary review, that America is about to see—has perhaps already seen—the birth of a new literary generation. The event is—or would be—momentous in a country like ours. New generations in France occur regularly by the calendar at intervals of three years. New generations in America occur reluctantly and after long delay like the gestations of the elephant. The difference is not so much due to racial distinctions as to distinctions in the use of words. A French generation is a manifesto and a new Movement. An American generation is an altered art. To test the truth of the happy expectation in the American, as opposed to the continental, sense it is therefore necessary to inquire whether an alteration of the literary art—or more specifically of the poetic art—has actually taken place. Now a change in an art is precisely what it purports to be—a change in an art. It is not merely a change in temper as from optimism to pessimism or from pessimism to optimism. It is not merely a change in subject matter as from love to economics or from classical archaeology to the frontier or from homily to revolution. It is something much more profound. The poet who uses the technique of Valéry or of Benét to write Communist propaganda is no more the founder of a new generation than is the poet who uses the technique of Eliot to assert resonantly that life is daisy. And no amount of critical hullabaloo from either end of the spectrum will suffice to build him to that posture. If subject matter and enthusiasm were all that mattered it would be enough to recall that both the cheerful neo-nationalist and the fervid neo-revolutionary find a prototype in Whitman and belong, if to any generation at all, to his.

The truth—the unhappy truth for the hopeful critic-mothers of these various broods—is that the deviations in the development of the art which we refer to as poetic generations are the effects not of the beliefs or the temperaments or the brags or the threats or the assertions of new poets but of their work. Pound is the authentic founder of the last American poetic generation not because Pound's economic and social and geographic opinions were different from those of his predecessors (the differences were generally unfortunate) but because Pound's *work* was different. There is precisely no substitute whatever for work. And nothing but work has generative power. A man may damn everything his predecessors did and still be impotent. A man may assert the opposite of the assertions of every man who has preceded him and still father no children. But if a man succeeds in producing work which has a new direction he will twist the road for all who come after him. Wherein that new direction will be felt is unpredictable and hopeless to define. A new technique may open to poetry a whole world from which it has been previously excluded or a new tone may profoundly alter the relation of the poet to *any* world. The important fact is that only successful work will show the way. It is not enough to assert in verse the merits of Marxism. It is not enough to assert in verse a vigorous belief in the beauty of existence. What is necessary in either case is to make the thing *happen* in the poem as it has never happened before. Which is not for a moment to suggest that the young men who are filled with hatred of the injustice and tawdriness and folly of capitalism or the young men who are filled with love of the land upon which they live are unimportant. Their importance on the contrary is of the first order. Out of the vigor of their emotions may well come a new art. But to mistake for the art the emotions is to perform no service to criticism. Only the art matters. The emotions light the stove.

It is for this reason that I find Agee's first book of more interest than any first book of poems I have seen for a long time. It will not excite the new-generationers, left wing or right. Agee does not assume what is usefully known as a Position. He obviously has a deep love of the land. Equally obviously he has a considerable contempt for the dying civilization in which he has spent twenty-four years. By both he comes honestly. He spent his boyhood, with his fair share of the disadvantages so generously bestowed by the not-quite-existing order, in and about the Cumberland Mountains, and some of his vacation time during his Harvard years he spent as a harvest stiff in the Kansas and Nebraska wheat fields. But neither emotion overrides his work and neither is capitalized to carry off the book. The whole emphasis is upon the work. And the work shows it. What appears is a technical apprenticeship successfully passed, a mature and in some cases a masterly control of rhythms, a vocabulary at once personal to the poet and appropriate to the intention and, above everything else, the one poetic gift which no amount of application can purchase and which no amount of ingenuity can fake—a delicate and perceptive ear. The book in other words is the book of a young poet laboring at an art rather than the book of a young poet laboring a distinction. And because the labor is severe and ardent and successful, because the poet is clearly recognizable in the labor, the book achieves an integral and inward importance altogether independent of the opinions and purposes of its author. What is always presented in the first work of any true artist is not an accomplishment but an instrument. The instrument which has been exercised in the making of these poems is one which is capable of enduring work.

Archibald MacLeish

Contents.

Foreword by Archibald MacLeish	5
I. Lyrics	11
II. Dedication	16
III. Ann Garner	24
IV. A Chorale	36
V. Epithalamium	38
VI. Sonnets	46
VII. Permit Me Voyage	59

I. Lyrics.

CHILD, should any pleasant boy
    Find you lovely, many could,
    Wind not up between your joy
The sly delays of maidenhood:

Spread all your beauty in his sight
And do him kindness every way,
Since soon, too soon, the wolfer night
Climbs in between, and ends fair play.

A SUMMER noon the middle sun
    Stunned me full of waking sleep
    And spread me slack as stone upon
The grass in water foundered deep

There in that steep and loaded shine
Of hungriest life and crested year
To dream what plenitudes were mine
What fat futurities made near

When cold athwart these ripening plans
The shade o'erswam me like a sheet
Of draughty disappointed vans,
And lobbered beak, and drawling feet.

NO doubt left. Enough deceiving.
    Now I know you do not love.
    Now you know I do not love.
Now we know we do not love.
No more doubt. No more deceiving.

Yet there is pity in us for each other
And better times are almost fresh as true.
The dog returns. And the man to his mother.
And tides. And you to me. And I to you.
And we are cowardly kind the cruellest way,
Feeling the cliff unmorsel from our heels
And knowing balance gone, we smile, and stay
A little, whirling our arms like desperate wheels.

NOT met and marred with the year's whole turn of grief,
But easily on the mercy of the morning
Fell this still folded leaf:

Small that never Summer spread
Demented on the dusty heat;
And sweet that never Fall
Wrung sere and tarnished red;
Safe now that never knew
Stunning Winter's bitter blue
It fell fair in the fair season:

Therefore with reason
Dress all in cheer and lightly put away
   With music and glad will
This little child that cheated the long day
   Of the long day's ill:
Who knows this breathing joy, heavy on us all,
   Never, never, never.

A Song.

I HAD a little child was born in the month of May.
He croaked and he crowed from early in the day.
He sang like a bird and he delighted to play
And before the night time he was gone away.

Little child, take no fright,
In that shadow where you are
The toothless glowworm grants you light.
Sure your mother's not afar.

Brave, brave, little boy,
Angels wave you round with joy.
Soon through the dark she runs to you,
Soon, soon your mother comforts you.

Description of Elysium.

There: far, friends: ours: dear dominion:

WHOLE health resides with peace,
    Gladness and never harm,
    There not time turning,
Nor fear of flower of snow

Where marbling water slides
No charm may halt of chill,
Air aisling the open acres,
And all the gracious trees

Spout up their standing fountains
Of wind-beloved green
And the blue conclaved mountains
Are grave guards

Stone and springing field
Wide one tenderness,
The unalterable hour
Smiles deathlessness:

No thing is there thinks:
Mind the witherer
Withers on the outward air:
We can not come there.

SURE on this shining night
  Of starmade shadows round,
  Kindness must watch for me
This side the ground.

The late year lies down the north.
All is healed, all is health.
High summer holds the earth.
  Hearts all whole.

Sure on this shining night I weep for wonder wandering far
    alone
Of shadows on the stars.

NOW thorn bone bare
  Silenced with iron the branch's gullet:
  Rattling merely on the air
Of hornleaved holly:

The stony mark where sand was by
The water of a nailèd foot:
The berry harder than the beak:
The hole beneath the dead oak root:

All now brought quiet
Through the latest throe
Quieted and ready and quiet:
Still not snow:

Still thorn bone bare
Iron in the silenced gully
Rattling only of the air
Through hornleaved holly.

The Happy Hen.

(To Dr. Marie Stopes et al, and to all scientific lovers)

HIS hottest love and most delight
   The rooster knows for speed of fear
   And winds her down and treads her right
And leaves her stuffed with dazzled cheer,

Rumpled allwhichways in her lint,
Who swears, shrugs, redeems her face,
And serves to mind us how a sprint
Heads swiftliest for the state of grace.

I LOITERED weeping with my bride for gladness
   Her walking side against and both embracing
   Through the brash brightening rain that now the season
     changes
White on the fallen air that now my fallen
                         the fallen girl her grave effaces.

II. Dedication.

*in much humility
to God in the highest
in the trust that he despises nothing.*

And in his commonwealth:

TO those who in all times have sought truth and who have told it in their art or in their living, who died in honor; and chiefly to these: Christ: Dante: Mozart: Shakspere: Bach: Homer: Beethoven: Swift: the fathers of Holy Scripture: Shelley: Brahms: Rembrandt: Keats: Cezanne: Gluck: Schubert: Lawrence: Van Gogh: and to an unknown sculptor of China, for his god's head.

To those of all times who have sought truth and who failed to tell it in their art or in their lives, and who now are dead.

To those who died in the high and humble knowledge of God: seers of visions; watchmen, defenders, vessels of his word; martyrs and priests and monarchs and young children and those of hurt mind; and to all saints unsainted.

To those unremembered who have died in no glory of peace, nor hope nor thought of any glory: to those who died in sorrow, and in kindness, and in bravery; to those who died in violence suddenly, and to all that saw not death upon them; to those who died awake to the work of death; to those who died in the dizziness of many years, not knowing their children for theirs; to those who died virgin, or barren; to those who died in the time of the joy of their strength; to those who took their own lives into the earth; to those who died in deadly sin.

To those who in their living time were frustrate with circumstance, and disadvantage; to those who died in the still desire of truth who never knew truth, nor much beauty, and small joy but the goodness of endurance; to all those who in all times have labored in the earth and who have wrought their time blindly, patient in the sun: and to all the dead in their generations:

And especially to Joel Tyler, and to James Agee my brave father, and to Jessie Tyler that became Mother Mary Gabriel, faithful maidservant of the most high God, and to Emma Farrand, the wife of Joel Tyler.
May they rest.

To those who, living, are soon to die: and especially to Via my wife, and to my mother, and to my sister Emma and to David Preston her husband, and to Gladys Lamar Agee my father's mother; and to Hugh Tyler, and to Paula Tyler, and to Erskine Wright, priest.

And to James Harold Flye, priest, who befriended my boyhood with the wisdom of gentleness, and to Grace his wife; to Edwin Clark Whitall, priest, patient in all his life; to Dorothy Carr; to the leniency and wisdom of four men, and to the scorn of another, who teach at Exeter Academy; to Theodore Spencer, in gratefulness; in love, to Arthur Percy Saunders and to his wife Louise and to their children; and to a dozen friends, who know their names.

To Mark Twain; to Walt Whitman; to Ring Lardner; to Hart Crane; to Abraham Lincoln; and to my land and to the squatters upon it and to their ways and words in love; and to my country in indifference.

To the guts and to the flexing heart and to the whole body of this language in much love, in grief for my dulness and in shame for my smallness and meagreness and caution. May I in time become as worthy of it as man may become of his words.

To those living and soon to die who tell truth or tell of truth, or who honorably seek to tell, or who tell the truths of others: especially to James Joyce; to Charles Spencer Chaplin; to Ivor Armstrong Richards; to Archibald MacLeish; to William Butler Yeats; to Pablo Picasso; to Albert Edward Housman; to Stephen Spender; to Roy Harris; to Albert Einstein; to Frederick Burrhus Skinner; to Walker Evans; to Diego Rivera; to Orozco; to Ernest Hemingway; to Scott Fitzgerald; to Arturo

Toscanini; to Yehudi Menuhin; to Irvine Frost Upham; to Robert Fitzgerald.

To those who know God lives, and who defend him.
To those who know the high estate of art, and who defend it.
To those who apprehend the dread of the magnitude of the destinies, and of the common conduct, of human kind, above all things known or earthly sought: and who as their hearts are able live toward the glory of the beauty, and in the shadow of the fear.
To those who suspect in every man, in the instant of his getting and thenceforward, how he is dignified among created creatures, how in him the world's whole harm and the world's whole good are met in the breath of God: and how in that instant he is given a mind to know and, though he be all one mechanism, freedom in his conduct before his creator.
To those who likewise suspect that hunger insatiable of the keeping and the enlargement and the knowing of being wherein he is conceived, wherein he lives, which in its appetites he may somewhat govern, and whereby he is wholly governed in all his ways.
To those who, beholding what man is, for love and for grief of what man should and may never earthly be, detest into madness man as he is and was and shall be, and all his works.
To those wiser who do not despise man in his doom, nor in the nature of his nature.
To that nature of man in earth which out of man's necessitudes, and delusions of necessitude, has wrought the societies and the nations of man, and his laws, that make a whore of justice, and his labors in the soil, and his workings of metal and stone and fibre and fire and light to his good use, and the contrivance of his ornament and entertainment, and his ways of good conduct and politeness; and his sciences; and his philosophies, and his religions, and his arts: and which interweaved these in the troubles and the nobilities of the flesh, and made them all into a structure no generation may deface, or

destroy, but it will build again: so that in all the wraths of our hope and need we are compelled forward and forever newly into a same darkness of unperfect practice.

To that nature of man in earth which has wrought this time upon us.

To all pure scientists, anatomists of truth and its revealers; in scorn of their truth as truth; and in thanksgiving for their truth in its residence in truth.

To all scientists and inventors of convenience and rapidity, and ways of health: in thanksgiving for their reductions of human pain, and labor, and unhealth; and in scorn for the same: since in the right end of their busyness we would all be healthful and undesiring as animate stones.

To those men who, of all nations unhindered, to all nations faithless, make it their business to destroy concord and to incite war and to prolong it, for their profit in the commerce of armament: to those governors of nations who, in full knowledge of this, visit upon them neither punishment nor restriction nor disapproval, but are accomplices, exhorting and deceiving and compelling the men for whose good life they rule deliberately into death, and death's danger, and the shattering of flesh and spirit. Of these merchants and of these rulers may the loins thaw with a shrieking pain, and may there be slow nails in the skulls of each, and may lost winds of plague unspeakable alight like flies upon their flesh, here in this earth and by public arrangement, to the sweet entertainment of all men of good will: and in their death may the vengeance of God shock their flesh from their bones, and their bones off the air, and all that was of them be reduced to the quintessence of pain very eternal, from moment to moment more exquisite everlastingly, by a geometrical increase: unless by improbable miracle they repent themselves straightway and for good.

To those who will not see that there is a disease of cupidity, and love of the fatherland, and pride, and the good heat for valor, upon all human flesh, which builds these men their conveniences, and makes them easy of heart in murder as a grocer selling greens: and it is a disease which may hardly be cured.

To those who are sure they can cure it.

To those merchants dealers and speculators in the wealth of the earth who own this world and its frames of law and government, its channels of advertisement and converse and opinion and its colleges, and most that is of its churches, and who employ this race and feed off it: to those among these rulers and these owners, these shapers of general thought, who decry these merchants of war: that they examine curiously, and honestly into their own hearts, and see how surely and to what like extent they in themselves are blood-guilty; and how and in what manifold ways they are more subtly and terribly and vastly accountable than for life blood alone: and that they repent their very existence as the men they are, and change or quit it: or visit the just curse upon themselves.

To those who think that any, or much, or all this condition may be a little, or much, or wholly changed. And to those who think that any one man is wholly guilty.

To those who have been deluded of their dignity as men and of their good knowledge into the practise and advancement of transient matters: to those whom love, or despair, or mildness, or magnanimity, or greed; or cloudiness of mind congenital or premeditated; or the strict allegories of the scientists, have thus deluded.

And especially to those whose souls are enraged that have beheld those practised and gravely cumulated idiocies which, since this race began, have been committed of man on men, for personal avarice or for national aggrandisement, lawlessly and by sanction and process of law; idiot children of that voracity which is the living strength of all men, and which may be changed in its courses for good or ill but never one jot altered in itself; those idiocies which have ever been and ever will be and are most obscenely now strong in the distinguishment of man from man, and strong to secure man's hatred of man and his privation, and dulness and blindness to truth, and eternal condemnation to wretchedness and all disadvantage. To those who have seen or suffered this condition, and who are fooled into the hope that it may be essentially changed. And into the hope that the cleansing of this state or its demolition and the establishment of a state new forged, and all discoveries of science applied, will do any greater service to man than to level and ameliorate the agonies and the exigencies of his living, to his ease, and into the ignorance of a contentment in earth and in the stuffs of the earth: to the blinding of his heart still further toward right knowledge of himself, and to the exasperation of those real agonies unbeheld, and in no time well beheld, of his ignorance before the mask of his destiny and before his God, where no knowledge nor ease of earth may help him.

And, knowing well that in this earth society, and law, and industry are the natural and indispensable necessities of man's earthly doom, earnestly to the hope (which can not be hope) that from this overthrow and change to come shall arise a race which, knowing concord in earth's least noisome commonwealth, may likewise know humility before God.

To those who will not watch into the mere shadow of death and behold the supremacy of man's ignorance over all man's knowledge. To those who will not see that there in that shadow is truth. To those who will not watch toward it, valuing it above all things in earth and valuing all things of earth in the thought of it.

To those among the murdering class who intend, and understand, no evil. To those among the murdered who grieve that they will murder many innocent men.

To all those who labor.

To those many who are indifferent to all semblance of truth; and to those millions who fear and detest it, and whom no change of state shall change.

To those who would not tell truth merely, but clearly in the hearts of all this people: for they crown a great impossibility, for which to die, with a mean crown and impossibility, and are somewhat mistaken.

To Leopold Bloom, and in his mildheartedness to all mankind.

To those who would be kind, and live quietly in the joy of their peacefulness.

To those who are more evil than kind.

To those dubious of evil, and of good.

To those who too surely distinguish them.

To those who have built this time in the earth in all its ways and who dwell in it variously as they may or must: farmers and workers and wandering men and builders and clerks and legislators and priests and doctors and scientists and governors of nations and engineers and prisoners and servants and sailors and merchants and soldiers and airmen and artists: in cities amassed, and on wide water, and lonesome in the air, and dark under the earth, and laboring in the land, and in materials, and in the flesh, and in the mind, and in the heart: knowing little and less of great and little matters: enduring all things and most enduring living, each in his way of patience, who all, surely as a brook slopes into a deep cave and is lost, must die, into what destiny not one may know: to all these who live and who must die and to those whom they breed to follow them in the earth to live and endure and breed and die: to the earth itself in its loveliness, and in all this race has done to it: and to its substance, and to its children every one, quick or quiet:

And to that space and darkness of sky beyond conjecture and to the coastless coasts that curb it if any there be such and to the whirling fires and the dead stones of the sky in their progressions upon the dark:

To the Holy Catholic and Apostolic Church and to the reach of its green boughs upon the sky through Godhead into Godhead, and to its branches withering and withered and fallen away:

And to that which, climbing the very sap, may deathly cling and blight that tree: in hatred, in grief, in faith:

To the entire hierarchy of the natural God, of every creature lone creator, in his truth unthinkable, undimensionable, endlessness of endlessness: beseeching him that he shall preserve this people.

O God, hear us.
O God, spare us.
O God, have mercy upon us.
Not one among us has seen you, nor shall in our living time, and may never. We fumble all blind on the blind dark, even who would know you and who believe your name. Our very faith and our desire, which are our whole and only way in truth, they delude us always, and ever will, into false and previous visions, and into wrong attributions. Little as we know beyond the sill of death do we know your nature: and the best of our knowledge is but a faith, the shade and shape of a dream, and all pretense.
Nevertheless have mercy upon us O great Lord God: for as there is some mercy, and the imaginations of nobleness, even in this your creature, surely, surely there is mercy in you and honor and sweet might: and a way to hear, and a way to see, and wisdom, and careful love. Have mercy upon us therefore, O deep God of the void, spare this race in this your earth still in our free choice: who will turn to you, and again fail you, and once more turn as ever we have done. And make the eyes of our hearts, and the voice of our hearts in speech, honest and lovely within the fences of our nature, and a little clear.

III. Ann Garner.

LIKE a stone set to mark a death, the bed
    Leaned through the leaping darkness, gaunt and square
    Against the firelight.
                    In her agony
Bent like a birch ice-laden, Ann Garner lay:
The silent woman by her in the dimness
Turned to the firelight, and said to the husband,
"She's laborin' hard; best set the plow beneath her."
Hips leant between the handles of the plow,
He thrust the flame-blue share beneath the bed.
And all the anguish flowed from her taut body,
Leaving her limp and silent in the darkness.
Then from the shadows the old woman walked,
Holding on rootlike hands the stillborn child.
The father drew the sheet to veil the eyes
That sought to pierce the leaping darkness where
Against the firelight, gaunt and square, the bed
Leaned like a stone set up to mark a death.

In harsh nakedness the earth upward thrusts
Its gaunt body, through the thin shroud of snow.
Above the rim of rocks, in the east,
Like a dull band of metal bends the dawn.
In the ice-clamped earth ring the shovels
And the ice-clamped earth leaps black
Against the sky.
                At the grave, Ann Garner
Holds the child, in a fleece close-wrapped,
Close-locked in a strong oak box.
In a strong oak box close-locked
They lower him into the frozen earth,
Lower him among the frozen roots.
The earth drums loud on the box.

Loud ring the shovels, and the wails
Of the women ring across the barren fields.
The mother stands silent by the grave.

    Here, on this height of pasture, where
    The wheeling sky and turning earth
    Convolute, grind;
    Here, at the universe's core,
    Here, on infinity's blind shore
    Let him lie buried.

    Here earth bereft again receives
    Into her open womb, her babe;
    Let the womb cohere:
    Let the flesh of her babe become her flesh,
    Let the blood of the babe to the hidden wells
    Of life drain downward.

    Let him live in womb and womb of earth;
    In the swelling seed of every plant
    Let him live.
    Let him distil on rising mists,
    Let him be blown along the sky,
    Let him rise through womb and womb of light;
    With stars at their birth
    Let him again be born.

High in the dark looms of the sky, the wind
With gentle hands wove a fine web of snow
Which from those silent fingers flowed in silence
Downward, to trail across the stony hills,
Downward, to settle over the black fields.
And now about Ann, the white-shrouded fields
Swept outward into an oblivion
Of whiteness. On every side an even whiteness
Was all that Ann could see, save where the wind
Laid bare and dreadful some black, angled stone.

That night her husband held her in his arms,
Spoke a few broken words, and in the darkness
Waited in sorrowful silence for the weeping
That he could better bear and better comfort
Than speechless grief. But at his side she lay,
The white snows falling, falling in her soul,
Blinding her grief save where some twisted stratum
Of her soul's framework thrust up bare and black.
And thus she sat throughout the winter days,
Holding her grief within her as a woman
Carrying a child unborn cradles its presence,
And sits apart in silence, cherishing
Its unborn life in joyful solitude.
Her husband would sit in sorrow, watching her;
Watching her daily slip a little farther
From his desire, and sympathy, and love.

A few days later, answering his call,
The midwife came once more to minister
To Ann, in whom the unsuckled milk had curdled.
Down to the pond's edge the old woman led them,
Jeff with an axe and shovel. "Now start diggin',"
She said, "An' keep on diggin' till ye strike
The muck. Ye're sure to find one hereabouts."
He shoveled off the snow, and with the axe
Chopped out the ice. Kneeling, the woman peered
About, and with her fingers clawed aside
The frozen reeds. There, in the splintered ice
And twisted roots, she found a frog, frozen.
Cupping it in her hands, she blew upon it,
The white breath streaming from her twisted fingers,
Until life stirred within him. "Open yer bodice,"
She murmured. And Ann bared her aching breasts.
Then, holding by two legs the frog, she suddenly
Jerked, and the frog hung throbbing, torn asunder.
Against Ann's breasts she laid the trembling flesh.

That night Ann left her husband's side, and stole
Out to the barn. Through the warm dimness surged
The lantern light, and in the light she saw
The plow. She stood a moment, very still;
Then, grasping the smooth, lantern-shining handles,
And between the handles leaning, through the chaff
Deep-sifted on the floor, she pushed the point,
Webbing the dust with strange significance.
Deep in the barn a restless hoof struck wood.
Ann left the plow, and holding high the lantern
That shed the light in dipping circles round her,
She stopped before the stall where the black bull
Stood breathing silver mist into the darkness.
The heat rolled out against her from his body
As, wondering at the gigantic power
Low-swung and latent on those wide-spread legs,
Staring, she reached out with an eager palm,
And laid it, for a moment, on his body . . .
Then, with a shudder, drew her hand away,
And ran, with the lantern sucking all the light
From the warm barn, and from the stamping cattle.

After that night Ann was more strange and silent
Even than formerly. Through the steel-blue dusk
That joined so closely night with winter night,
She would sit spinning in the chimney corner,
The white thread flowing round the polished wheel,
The white snow falling, falling in her soul . . .
The ice thinned outward from the banks; the ice
Thawed upon birches pitifully bent.
From upland pasture the cold winter sky
Lifted its weight. And yet Ann sat and spun.
Always her eyes, dull as two stones, were fixed
On the white circle streaming through the darkness.
Thus passed the dim short days; and then in silence

Drawing the sheet to veil her eyes, she lay
Upon the bed which leaned against the firelight
Like a dark stone set to mark a death.

One night Ann woke, and, ear pressed to the darkness,
Knew that the world was called again to life.
Life poured against the walls in silent torrents . . .
The walls of wood, that locked her close within them!
She sprang up, and ran out into the night,
Blind in her running. Through the hissing pines
And out upon that naked lift of pasture
Where lay her stillborn child, she came, and there
Was caught in the wash and welter of two waves
Of life. From field and forest life welled upward,
And from the sky life fell like streaming rain
And lay upon the earth in a black flood.
Over the rock-rimmed pasture heights, the stars
Poured through the sky, and earthward from the sky
Struck silver rods of starlight, in black prisms
Of night.   Ann stood a moment, hands upraised,
Then sank upon the grave, her body tense
Against the earth. And there she lay until
Dawn's white sun-bladed wings soared up the east.
Then standing up, beneath her feet she saw
Fields rear their arched brown backs above the mists,
Saw the wild foaming green on every tree.
She saw black cattle moving through the dawn
Up heights of pasture. Through the spreading dawn
Leaped a wild, silver wind, that circled round her,
Then gathered all its power and blew against
And through her, whipping her joy-maddened body
Into the riot and revel of its dance.

Now the blue plowshare surged in the broad fields,
The black earth, riven by the flame-like blade,

In sinuous furrows flowed behind. Ann watched
The plunging and inexorable plow,
Watched her husband guiding it, and when
The work was done, and over the quiet hills
The sky glowed greenly, stealing out alone,
Ann pressed her body to the raw, rich earth
And felt life swelling great against locked stones.
As the fields grew toward grandeur of the harvest,
Ann walked in silent joy through the tall grain
Silver and shadowy in the shifting wind,
Or stood beneath the dip of apple-boughs,
Long fingers searching out the ripening fruit
Let down in heaviness through clasp of leaves.

Now in the fields men cradled flashing scythes
Slanting in unison close to the ground.
The wheat sank ripe and rustling, and the women
Following, swept it up in golden armfuls,
Binding it on their hips.
                        But Ann stood by,
Chained to the earth by the ripe, gold grain,
Her body towering in the gold sunlight
Above the crash of wind-bewildered grain,
Above the harvest-work of man and metal.

On windy nights the apples thundered down.
The fields grew hard and black as the cold crept
Little by little down the bitter sky.
Ann saw the trees bleed on the earth their leaves,
And saw the rose-bush cower against the trellis,
And saw the rose lock all its life and color
Within a bitter berry, tremulous
On the bare bramble, in the icy wind.
She took her child and buried him again
High on the pasture, under the cold stars,
And bent her body to the whirring wheel.

When in the high looms of the windy sky
Fine veils of snow were woven and blew out
Above the naked fields, then in her soul
Fell the white snow, the blind and soothing snow.

* * * * * * *

As the years passed, the people turned to Ann
In doubt about some matter of their planting.
For with the years, Ann seemed to grow more learned
In all the mysteries of darkened moons,
Of hidden wells. And always at a birth
Silent and skilled she bent above the bed.
Always she moved among them like a ghost,
Her eyes as dull and fixed as two round stones.
But while the people round her bent their backs
Beneath the inexorable scourge of age,
Her body gained in stature and in strength,
Becoming every spring a little richer,
More flowing in its grace. And when alone,
Her eyes were still as water beneath mist.

All through the winter days she sat alone,
Spinning the white thread round the dark wood wheel;
At night she lay sometimes beside her husband,
Silent and grey and bitter, and more often
She stole out to the barn, and gazed about her
At all the symbols of the black earth's yield—
Plow, scythe, harrow—and lay down
To sleep among them, with the stamping cattle.
In winter she was never seen outdoors,
But locked her grief within the cabin's dimness.

                              But on the night
When Spring and Winter overlapped great wings
High in the sky, and like two eagles fought
For dominance below, she would run out
Into the flooding winds. And after that

She scarcely lived within the cabin's walls,
But with the cattle moving up the mountain
She walked along the streaming mists of dawn,
Until beneath the sun they burned to nothingness;
Then in the swaying dimness of the forest
She lay beneath the gnarled mountain laurel
Or on the cool and calm of fallen oak leaves,
And heard the rush of wind among the leaves,
The subtle writhe and shiver of an earth
Forever tortured by the myriad roots
Sprawling in darkness downward. And at night,
When the sheep whitely streamed down the bare hills,
When darkness welled down the wide peaceful sky,
And silence mourned over the misty earth,
She rose, and from the height of naked pasture
Watched the stars slowly swing across the sky,
Or brooded above the dark, wide fields that flowed
Into the starlight, cradling the life
That blindly moved within.

      Life was in death:
The world rolled black and barren in its mists,
And life was locked deep in the sheathing snows;
Then wind and sun and rain came, like a lover,
Clasping the world in fierce, caressing arms,
And on her body lying, warm and undulant;
And all life sprang to meet him.

      And with life
Of her own life thus given each year's rebirth,
Ann came to look upon herself as earth,
And lying strained against the earth, cried out
In joy at sweeping winds, at the warm sun,
At the black rain that plunged into the earth.
And thus, as the years passed, she lost the rhythms
That govern human life, and seemed to live

More like a tree, or like the earth itself.
The only intercourse with humankind
She held, was at a childbirth or a funeral,
Or in the spring, when all the people turned
Toward her to guide them in their planting. Then
With strange serenity she moved among them,
Handling the simple farming implements
Like sacred symbols of fertility.

As long as Ann lived, all the countryside
Was rich in produce—as long as Ann lived.

* * * * * * *

Ann never would have died within four walls,
Her body stretched beneath a fear-clutched sheet.
She never could have died, save in some great
Catastrophe of all the universe.

On a night in moon-dark, all the people stood
Silent and fearful, at the soil's first breaking.
The horses loomed against the starry sky,
And Ann, behind them, stood a minute, gazing
Across the black earth, and the shrinking snows.
Then, grasping the curved handles of the plow,
She poised the point against the earth, and pushed.
The horses started forward, and the earth
Rolled back before the darkly gleaming blade.
Then, stepping silently along the furrow,
With a wide-sweeping arm she cast out grain,
And once more stood in silence, staring out
Across the windblown fields, the windblown stars.

Next morning, all the preachers of the country
Saddled their horses, rode to every cabin,
Stood in the doorway, clenching in white knuckles
A roll of scripture, and forewarned the people
That in the darkened moon, only two nights

From then, all in the dread of God should gather
To greet, amidst fearsome falling of the stars,
The blasting of evil and the doom of earth.
And all the people swarmed down the ravines,
And crowded the frame churches, and began
Even in early dusk, to wail and sing
And pray, and hear the preacher's exhortations.

Ann lay half sinking in the fragrant needles
Fallen beneath the pines. Above her rose
The pasture, straining toward darkening sky.
Faint upon the crest she could discern
The higher grass beneath which lay her child.
The pines hissed softly in the evening breeze,
And in the clear sky, one by one, the stars
Burned through. From far below in the valley
The slow bells of returning flocks rang out.
Then darkness, like a slow wind in the sky,
Settled upon the hills—
                     Down through the sky
A star streamed, like a golden rod that split
In half the darkness.

                Ann sprang to her feet
And, running to the highest crest of pasture,
Stood, staring out across the world. Another
And yet another, and again a star
Streaked downward. All the heavens seemed to slip
And swoop and shuttle, weaving a wild web
Of gold across the sky. And then, through all,
Fell a great, burning sphere, and myriad stars
Around it.—
   Sweeping above her wide black fields,
   Rending screaming air asunder,
   Into fields glowing stars
   Plunge with roll and groan of thunder.

Down wide skies the golden plow
Riving, cleaves a flaming furrow
Wide for the seeds of a greater sowing.
Whence comes the sower? Along the furrow

Striding great upon the sky,
Sweeping wide a flaming hand,
He sows the universe anew,
Advancing toward her pasture-land,
Arms flexed above her, blotting the sky
With body bent to the world's rim. . . .

* * * * * * *

Her husband found her on the heave of earth
Beneath which lay her child, in six oak boards
Tight-locked against the earth. Ann's hair was blown
Back from the hollow temples, in a way
To mould the head in savage eagerness
Which bent her body into one taut curve.

Clawing in jealousy at his swept beard,
He pondered the chisellings of lust
That so transformed in death the woman who
Had lived beside him silent as a ghost.
Then seeing that the clothes torn from her body
Were clenched in her own hands, he made all haste
To bury her before his neighbors, coming
And staring at that flared and joyful mouth,
Should nudge and whisper, and believe the thing
He knew could not be true. So, from his cabin
Returning with a shovel, he began
To dig, fearing to question the lustful mask.

He dug down through the grave where, years before,
His shovel rang out in the ice-clamped earth,
And digging, struck the box. He pried it open
And strangely gazed upon the fleece that wrapped

His child. Then, lifting in his arms his wife,
He lowered her among the broken roots,
And starting to replace the little box,
Stopped. From the fleece he clutched the crumbled bones,
And in Ann Garner's mouth he sprinkled bones,
And on Ann Garner's eyes he sprinkled bones—

Then gently laid the earth above her body,
And looked about him at the windswept dawn,
And slowly through the trees walked to his cabin.

1928.

IV. A Chorale.

WHO, knowing love must die or live free-fated,
Free in your heartsearth headlong man created:
Who manly died and sealed from all perdition
    Our ill condition:

Your crown not God nor your great death retains you:
As you are man so man for man ordains you:
Who reign in man's regard O much forsaken
    Dear Christ awaken!

Range the blest hordes that rest in you around you:
Look down kind prince on treason to astound you:
See now sweet farmer what a wasting shadow
    Takes your green meadow:

How, love of self, fact, state, and art much prizing,
Men move in manners of their own devising:
How they kill truth to find out truth more nearly
    That's mortal merely:

How knowledge muffles wisdom's eye to danger:
How greed misrules: how greed's enraged avenger
Swears greed the equal prize for man's pursuing,
    And your undoing:

How many ways men build up man's disaster:
How all are armaments against man's master:
How surely soon comes toward without atonement
    Your disenthronement:

How cowardly those few that still exalt you
Worship their death while wildly men assault you:
How not one dares who knows what men intend you,
    Die to defend you:

Though you outreign our time which is an hour,
Yet you in us have put you in our power:
What God man builds in God His truth is ended
      Not well defended:

O Godsent Son of God our allsalvation,
Is faith so sickly slow to indignation
Your murderers against? Then faith betrays you:
      Your friends destroy you:

Your faith who gave your heart for our safekeeping,
Your love who sweated blood while we were sleeping,
If so these waste within this generation
      Death is your nation:

The time is withered of your ancient glory:
Your doing in this sweet earth a pretty story:
O noblest heart fare well through the conclusion
      Of all delusion.

Great God kind God the deep fire-headed fountain
Of earth and funneled hell and hopeful mountain:
Of ghosted Gods the eversame survivor:
Of shoreless strength of peace the prime contriver:
If this your Son is now indeed debasèd
Among old effigies of Gods effacèd,
Blaze in our hearts who still in earth commend you:
Who through all desolation will defend you:
For we are blinded all and steep are swervèd
Far among many Deaths who still would be preservèd.

V. Epithalamium.

I.

NOW day departs: Upreared the darkness climbs
    The breathless sky, leans wide above the fields,
    And snows its silence round the muttering chimes:
The night is come that bride to bridegroom yields.

The night is come, that hallows as it harms,
That in perfection clothes the flesh defaced.
Now let the mother gather in her arms
The body that to other arms must haste.

For lo: from Oeta's wild and windflayed height
A star takes wing, soars up the wide arched sky.
And, from the constant fountain crest of flight,
Lowers on the marriage bed its prospering eye.

Still, with the glad impatient waiting o'er,
Weeping, with weak embrace, the mother shields
The maiden who is hers to guard no more:
The night is come, that bride to bridegroom yields.

II.

Thick through the blended darkness slow-born dews distil,
Swell upon stem and stone, confuse the night.
Toward Hesperus still gazing poised fond above the hill
Now wind the glad torch flames, full blown and bright.

Soft through the sleeping meadows blind with dark and dew
We move, our torches shaking off the gloom.
We maim the soundless woodland, we bear our drenched yew,
We come to the marriage bed, the waiting groom.

III.

Hesperus alone holds all the windworn sky,
Involves the bed in his steep, streaming light;
And dusts that ever in aloofness lie
Shudder to life, and marvel at the night.

For from the sky now falls a holy dower
Over the subtle ruin of her charms,
And the mute dusts, that swell with Hesperus' power,
Shall hold her joys and shield from all alarms.

IV.

How proud in gentle modesty she lies
And greets her lover with stately tenderness.
No wanton glance, no false coquettish sighs
Betray her love, her sober eagerness.

No smile she grants, no blushes red confuse
Her pure flesh in its white tranquillity:
Quiet on her bed amid the glancing dews,
Queenly she waits in rich humility.

V.

For that he, in whose arms you soon shall lie,
Not without guilt comes to a guiltless bride,
Still fear him not, but tender at his side
Recall his sorrow and his deep distress,
Recall his loneliness.

No boy has lived, but he has been his friend,
No maiden but has lain within his arms.
Hopeful of love fulfilled, he sought their charms,
But all the visions that his full heart cherished
In short time perished.

Through the dark depths of ocean and of sky,
Through all the world he pursued his endless quest,
And gathered every beauty to his breast:
But found no love, and sought on, unavailing,
His hope fast failing.

Now, with this night, his search is at an end.
The myriad blemished beauties you assumed,
That long were dead, late in enchantment bloomed.
Now, knowing all love and joy in you alone,
He takes you for his own.

So, wound him not with one misgiving sigh;
With his clear rapture let no sorrow blend.
Lo, holy Hesperus watches from on high,
His still fires round your lover's heart descend
And to rude passion put an end.

VI.

Now the groom joins her, and the happy lovers
Bind heart to heart with close-encircling arms.
Hesper's clear benediction round them hovers;
The night is come that hallows as it harms.

O maids, through whose translucent masks of grief
Envious gladness gleams, for all her charms
Outshine your own, nay, Beauty's, past belief,
Your night will come, that hallows as it harms.

And youths, whose loving eyes feast and delay,
Though hope is gone, and holy vows are sealed,
Put off your sorrow, woo but for a day,
And night will come, and bride to bridegroom yield.

Over the lovers and the marriage bed,
Bare to the staring sky, the chilling dew,
Now close protection and concealment spread,
Clod upon branch, soft dust and sacred yew.

VII.

Let no noise born of night come near their room:
No milk-eyed frog, with bubble-throated croaks,
Nor screaking bat, whose wings hook through the gloom,
Nor mournful owl, whose lost and dreary yell
The monstrous deities of the dark invokes.

Let no foul mist that cold above them trails
Settle upon them, smothering wrap them round.
But venom that the sweltering marsh exhales
Loose-coiled and prowling, let the wind confound
And in the dry blast let its damp be drowned.

Let them lie safe: from every evil spell
That witches chant to sour true lovers' joys,
From the lank spirits night recalls from hell,
From ghost that gibbers, and from ghoul that wails,
From all malevolence the night employs.

It stands not in our narrow realm of power
To ward off aught that ever joy has marred,
But put off fear, for from this blessed hour
The stars, the sky, and all the earth, stand guard.

Root clenches root, dust into hard earth blends;
With bolts of stone the door's forever barred;
Across the wounded hill the long grass mends;
Around the lovers all the earth stands guard.

The twelve thongs of the wind shall lash and shred
The mists to air, shall soften, and retard,
And droop a rainy curtain round the bed:
Over the lovers all the sky stands guard.

Hesperus marshals all his myriad throng:
Down the deep night they gaze, with fond regard
And fateful, who shall shield them from all wrong:
Over the lovers all the stars stand guard.

VIII.

'Tis time that we, who loved her through the day,
Whom Hesperus is urgent to bereave,
No longer should their rightful joys delay,
But fondly and forever take our leave.

Even now in tenderness the lovers pause,
And, for a moment, all is blind as night,
All, save their love, that, the next moment, draws
Them on to realms of measureless delight.

Knotted in secrecy, the sacred zone
From every harm the unharmed virgin shields:
One may unloose the knot, and one alone:
The night is come, and bride to bridegroom yields.

Close in her kindly and untroubled arms,
He sets the zone aside, with gentle haste:
The night is come, that hallows as it harms,
And she assumes perfection, who was chaste.

Flesh and bright flesh he draws from off his bride:
Dust holds her wedding garment with the zone.
He who sets carnal nakedness aside
Knows the blank final bareness of the bone.

Now all is ready, now the happy bride
Lies unclothed as her lover, and on love
That long frustration and the zone denied,
Hesperus streams his sanction from above.

Now she yields all: her body to his own,
Her steadfast loving gaze, her mouth to his kiss—
All beauty and all love has never known
The ragged shadow of their radiant bliss.

Their love burns wilder, and the steady brand
Flares into furious and holy lust.
Their substance shivers and runs down like sand
Into the dust, and is one with the dust.

IX.

For that the flesh arises like a wall
Between two souls, all love has known distress.
But they have conquered sorrow, conquered all
That clouded love: are one in nothingness.

Such nothingness remains, and yet is gone,
Looks upon all, and yet is void of sight,
Quickens the roots of every flowering dawn,
Coils in the core of every ripening night:

It breathes from steady water, is the pain
Of bursting seeds, the agony of earth
Shuddering out its life; streams down in rain
That causes and alleviates all birth:

X.

When spring returns:—with every spring to come,
When the black worldseed buds and is full blown,
When all is singing that was frozen dumb,
Behold her children, whom no man has known!

When the long hill-grass hisses and interlaces,
When the tree stands aloof that split the stone,
When the leaves greenly stream in the wind-mad places,
Behold her children whom no man has known!

She who lies at the bottom of the night,
She who was flesh ere flesh revealed the bone
And bone relaxed to dust is deathless light:
And such her children whom no man has known!

XI.

But still we stand, and they are scarce abed.
Scarce has their long and joyful night begun.
Now at their door the last yew branches spread
And hasten home; for night is nearly done.

Unformed and grey, heavy with lingering night,
Soft in its solitude stoops every tree.
All is submerged and blurred in fragile light
As at the bottom of a moonled sea.

Dispread among the hills, bemused and wan
Lie the night tarnished half awakened fields.
The stars shrink back on white oblivion:
The dim sky loosens, and the long night yields.

Over the rim of mountains in the east
The daybreak, that through all the hours of night
Welled steady from the nadir, now, released,
Floods all the earth and sky with glassy light.

Wind flaws the shifting grandeur of the grain,
Pours through the green confusion of the leaves.
The mists become as air, our torches wane:
And once more Hesperus his dark hill perceives.

His strong and bright protection is as naught:
O'er lovers whom no darkness would dismay
O'er all enchantment that the night has wrought,
Merciless storms the overwhelming day.

XII.

Quiet, forever free from all alarms,
They lie where light is strengthless to descend.
The night is come, that hallows as it harms:
The night is come that day may never end.

1930.

VI. Sonnets.

I.

SO it begins. Adam is in his earth
   Tempted, and fallen, and his doom made sure
   O, in the very instant of his birth:
Whose deathly nature must all things endure.
The hungers of his flesh, and mind, and heart,
That governed him when he was in the womb,
These ravenings multiply in every part:
And shall release him only to the tomb.
Meantime he works the earth, and builds up nations,
And trades, and wars, and learns, and worships chance,
And looks to God, and weaves the generations
Which shall his many hungerings advance
When he is sunken dead among his sins.
Adam is in this earth. So it begins.

II.

OUR doom is in our being. We began
   In hunger eager more than ache of hell:
   And in that hunger became each a man
Ravened with hunger death alone may spell:
And in that hunger live, as lived the dead,
Who sought, as now we seek, in the same ways,
Nobly, and hatefully, what angel's-bread
Might ever stand us out these short few days.
So is this race in this wild hour confounded:
And though you rectify the big distress,
And kill all outward wrong where wrong abounded,
Your hunger cannot make this hunger less
Which breeds all wrath and right, and shall not die
In earth, and finds some hope upon the sky.

III.

THE wide earth's orchard of your time of knowing,
Shine of the springtime pleasures into bloom
And branchèd throes of health: but soon the snowing
And tender foretaste of your afterdoom,
Of fallen blossoming air persuades the air
In hardier practises: and soon dilate
Fruits and the air together that shall bear
Earthward the heavied boughs and to their fate:
Wrung of the wealth and wonder they unfurled
By that same air: which air the sun deranges
To slope the living season from the world
And charge the world with snow that all estranges.
Watch well this sun, and air, and orchard green:
None stay these changes every man has seen.

IV.

I HAVE been fashioned on a chain of flesh
Whose backward length is broken on the dust:
Frail though the dust and small as the dew's mesh
The morning mars, it holds me to a trust:
My flesh that was, long as this flesh knew life,
Strove, and was valiant, still strove, and was naught:
Now it is mine to wage their valiant strife
And failing seek still what they ever sought.
I have been given strength they never wore.
I have been given hope they never knew.
And they were brave, who can be brave no more.
And they that live are kind as they are few.
'Tis mine to touch with deathlessness their clay:
And I shall fail, and join those I betray.

V.

STRENGTHLESS they stand assembled in the shadow,
   Blind to all strife and all to sorrow blind
   Who reared the tower, who scored the April meadow:
Sheltered, they overshade my strengthless mind.
Those hands that gave their kind ungentle power
To summer's travail, autumn did not spare:
That mind which knew the clear, the intact hour,
Now is disparted on a changeful air.

The hands that ached to help are pithless bone
(Mind, mind, the harsh pain and the unalloyed:
What fruit you bear, that must you bear alone!)
The broken helmet nods around its void:
So I disclothe me of this shadow's blight;
And stand the axis of swift noon, sure night.

VI.

SEASON of change the sun for distaff bearing
   In your right hand and in the left large rains
   And writhen winds and noiselessly forth faring
The earth abroad, and streaming wide your skeins,
When in unfathomed fairness you have clothed
The sea with quiet, the land with painless wealth,
Turn you to those who changelessly have loathed
All and their kind, and grant them peace and health:
The proud stone-parting ardor of the tree,
The glee of ice relaxed against new earth,
Joy of the lamb and lust of bloom-struck bee
Grant to the sick, stiff, spiteful, like fresh birth.
Let this new time no natural wheel derange:
Be ever changeless, thus: season of change.

VII.

WHAT dynasties of destinies undreamed
    And truth to halt the heart does man descry
    There, that so rarely has his heart beteemed
His eye to frankly watch into an eye?
The earliest marvelings only of the heart
Estranged of blindness of its living care
And from beholding Being held athwart
By narrowest shade, so deeply make him dare.
What truth we glimpse that each see other so
That stills our blood with horror of delight
Which once alone with other each may know:
Who swiftly changed recoil from that dread sight:
And how, if that were told, would change this day:
All human kind has seen, and none can say.

VIII.

WHAT curious thing is love that you and I
    Hold it impervious to all distress
    And insolent in gladness set it high
Above all other joy and goodliness?
Ignorance and unkindness, aspiration,
The weary flesh, the mind's inconstancy,
Even now conspire its sure disintegration:
Be mindful, love, of love's mortality.
Be mindful that all love is as the grass
And all the goodliness of love the flower
Of grass, for lo, its little day shall pass
And withering and decay define its hour.
All that we hold most lovely, and most cherish
And most are proud in, all shall surely perish.

IX.

WHY am I here? Why do you look at me
    Triumphantly and lovingly and long?
    When were we captured? When shall I be free
From your delight and this delicious wrong?
Not by your will I trust, nor by my own
I swear, nor any close device of reason
Are we engulfed by thicker walls than stone,
Mismated victims of unfounded treason.
Forbear, forbear to look at me with joy.
I would not do you hurt who will no harm,
But that sure smile I surely shall destroy—
Its covert meaning and its patent charm.
Awakened to our love's surprising hell,
Your dream struck sleep befits it hardly well.

X.

WRING me no more nor force from me that vow
    Which lovers love to hear for reassurance;
    Rest faithful in firm silence, which is now
Frail but sole bulwark for our love's endurance.
However mad, it is my heart's belief
That he who lies of love trumpets instruction
For anger and terror, scorn and doubt and grief
Swiftly to marshal toward our sure destruction.
Since, though we know naught else, we know love true,
When from the strict course which love's truth affirms
The sick brain swerves, to guiltless hearts accrue
Love's penalties and unpalliable terms.
If you love truly, speak the vow for me:
My lips can ill afford the blasphemy.

XI.

FOR love departed, lover, cease to mourn.
Of flesh conceived, love fed upon our flesh
And of our agony and joy was born;
Whence often we have wept: weep not afresh.
How love grew strong and lovelier than we
Was all our joy, is for our solace still:
Woe though it was that wreck of strength to see
Thaw down and die, it was not by our will.
Our will? who sleepless and with anguished care
Plied every heartful balm and thoughtful cure,
Due rite of lust and precondemned prayer:
All which despite our love might not endure:
Because this forewrought evil has prevailed
Shall we mourn love and say that we have failed?

XII.

IS love then royal on some holy height?
Thence does he judge us, thence dispense his grace?
There strike apart the darkness and the light
And shroud in light his sight-destroying face?
What are his laws? By what high-dealt decrees
Do lovers snared by all the laws of earth
Transcend the pain and cruelty and lost ease
That globes our globe, and soar to heavenward birth?
I have known love as lowly, full of lust,
Bent on contriving Godhead from the flesh,
Wrought of desire and waning through mistrust,
Starved in the sinuately carnal mesh.
Is there indeed a God who can redeem
The love we know as a dawn-tinctured dream?

XIII.

SORROWFUL or angry, hold it no way remiss
   That, with the last gasp of love's healthless breath
   (More cruelly stopped than with our latest kiss)
I would dissuade you from my imminent death.
The heart knows love exanimate of reason,
And your love thus beyond all reason dead;
The astounded brain, incredulous of treason,
Still must defy what heartful hope has fled.
Though the deliberate autumn air bereaves
With curious raveling all the rich-wrought earth,
The stringent winter through some idiot leaves
Outbrave defeat until the new leaves' birth:
When only (should that dubious spring renew)
Dying to live, I'll know my heart was true.

XIV.

NOT of good will my mother's flesh was wrought,
   Whose parents sowed in joy, and garnered care:
   The sullen harvest sudden winter brought
Upon their time, outlasting their despair.
Deep of a young girl's April strength his own
My father's drank, and draughted her to age:
Who in his strength met death and was outdone
Of high and hopeless dreams, and grief, and rage.

Poor wrath and rich humility, these met,
Married, and sorrowing in a barren bed
Their flesh embraced in pity did beget
Flesh that must soon secure their fleshlihead:
But knows not when, on whom cannot descry,
And least of all could vaunt conjecture why.

XV.

BUT that all these, so hopeful of their day,
Highsouled in joy and hungry for the fight,
Loved all too well such loving to betray,
And linked in love declined into the night
Whose dusk is flesh, whose dark is family,
Whose midnight is despair full-wrought from love;
Despair of strength and the soul's entity;
Opposed to noon by this thick world's remove.

And since I burn so wrathfully with joy,
And love also, as kindly as did they,
And so would fight, and so would not destroy
Night-hearted love that shows so proud a day:
I'll choose the course my fathers chose before.
And, with their shadows, pray my son does more.

XVI.

HOW all a hurrying year was negligence,
Each meeting other as the casual merely,
In aimless fondness and the year's expense
Of much not seen and nothing sought sincerely:
Knowing such little truth, so lightly wearing
The small regrets of ill-established friends,
And our unmeasured liking meanly sharing,
And wanting yet evading all amends:

How, for all fear, that thing which dignifies
Our selves in each above those affable
So used its strength once that our helpless eyes
Killed and restored us in the fact in full:
How these things were, stuns and outstands my thought,
Now we are joined in all we scarcely sought.

XVII.

I NOTHING saw in you that was not common
In some degree to any other friend,
Nothing that any amiable woman
Might not possess or by her wit pretend:
Only that we were straggling in our speech,
Uneasy in our liking, much as though
There dwelt such content in the heart of each
As needs must speak, but how it did not know:
True, this seemed strange to me, as well it might,
And did to you, yet neither had the art
To guess the truth and certify the sight
To the perceptions of the powerless heart:
Which now our selves so powerfully convince,
All the world else is idiocy since.

XVIII.

THE way the cleansouled mirror of a soul
Dreams in the darkened flesh and smoky breath
That only takes and tells the image whole
When all obstruction's wiped away by death:
So with our hearts that sleeping long have dreamed
Imaginations of celestial love.
Their flaws in each the other has redeemed
(True lovers such obscurities remove).
And now, but slowly, see our hearts awake.
The eyes unshut, the living sight shine clear;
How still each heart reluctant lies to take
The image of its image: though so near
We lie, that surely both our hearts perceive
Identities they scarcely yet believe.

XIX.

THOSE former loves wherein our lives have run
    Seeing them shining, following them far,
    Were but a hot deflection of the sun,
The operation of a migrant star.
In that wrong time when still a shape of earth
Severed us far and stood our sight between,
Those loves were effigies of love whose worth
Was all our wandering nothing to have seen:
So toward those steep projections on our sky
We toiled though partners to their falsity
Who faintly in that falseness could descry
What now stands forth too marvelous to see:
Who one time loved in them the truth concealed:
And now must leave them in the truth revealed.

XX.

NOW stands our love on that still verge of day
    Where darkness loiters leaf to leaf releasing
    Lone tree to silvering tree: then slopes away
Before the morning's deep-drawn strength increasing
Till the sweet land lies burnished in the dawn:
But sleeping still: nor stirs a thread of grass:
Large on the low hill and the spangled lawn
The pureleaved air dwells passionless as glass:
So stands our love new found and unaroused,
Appareled in all peace and innocence,
In all lost shadows of love past still drowsed
Against foreknowledge of such immanence
As now, with earth outshone and earth's wide air,
Shows each to other as this morning fair.

XXI.

WHO but sniffs substance gorges it, my soul,
   Smothers digestion with stuffed appetite.
   Disorders work in him and he is whole
One swill of dreams that all ways wreak him spite.
As arsenic can make a plant seem fresh
So are these hoisted dreams that are the flesh
A health not his and false and neverlasting
But loved once known which blinds with change and wasting.
So by my birth are you: wherefore this wry,
This raw corrective that alone outwrings
These doubly deathful healths: so though we die
Yet so die not one coward but two kings.
So should we live, why then God lives also.
That was His Will which then will be our Woe.

XXII.

WHEN beyond noise of logic I shall know
   And in that knowledge swear my knowledge bound
   In all things constant, never more to show
Its head in any transience it has found:
When pride of knowledge, frames of government,
The wrath of justice gagged and greed in power,
Sure good, and certain ill, and high minds bent
On destiny sink deathward as this hour:
When deep beyond surmise the driven shade
Of this our earth and mind my mind confirms,
Essence and fact of all things that are made,
Nature in love in death are shown the terms:
When, through this lens, I've seen all things in one,
Then, nor before, I truly have begun.

XXIII.

THIS little time the breath and bulk of being
Are met in me: who from the eldest shade
Of all undreamt am raised forth into seeing
As I may see, the state of all things made:
In sense and dream and death to make my heart
Wise in the loveliness and natural health
Of all, and God, upon the void a part:
Likewise to celebrate this commonwealth:
Believing nothing, and believing all,
In love, in detestation, but most
In naught to sing of all: to recall
What wisdom was before I was this ghost:
Such songs I shall not make nor truths shall know:
And once more mindless into truth shall go.

XXIV.

SURE fortitude must disabuse my mind
Of all enlargements in unfounded hope
That I perceive whom fear of self made blind
My destiny constrained in my own scope.
All memory of magnificence of sound,
All grandeur and finality of word,
All nobleness some alien pain has found
That lives here painless, let them be interred.
Those men I worship and would stand among
In death well gained and reverently would greet,
Those immense souls have peopled mine too long,
And blown it broad with hope that was deceit:
And my poor soul, if aught it would create,
Must fast of these, and feed on its own fate.

XXV.

My sovereign souls, God grant my sometime brothers,
I must desert your ways now if I can.
I followed hard but now forsake all others,
And stand in hope to make myself a man.
This mouth that blabbed so loud with foreign song
I'll shut awhile, or gargle if I sing.
Have patience, let me too, though it be long
Or never, till my throat shall truly ring.

These are confusing times and dazed with fate:
Fear, easy faith, or wrath's on every voice:
Those toward the truth with brain are blind or hate:
The heart is cloven on a hidden choice:
In which respect I still shall follow you.
And, when I fail, know where the fault is due.

VII. Permit Me Voyage.

From the Third Voyage of Hart Crane.

TAKE these who will as may be: I
    Am careless now of what they fail:
    My heart and mind discharted lie
And surely as the nervèd nail

Appoints all quarters on the north
So now it designates him forth
My sovereign God my princely soul
Whereon my flesh is priestly stole:

Whence forth shall my heart and mind
To God through soul entirely bow,
Therein such strong increase to find
In truth as is my fate to know:

Small though that be great God I know
I know in this gigantic day
What God is ruined and I know
How labors with Godhead this day:

How from the porches of our sky
The crested glory is declined:
And hear with what translated cry
The stridden soul is overshined:

And how this world of wildness through
True poets shall walk who herald you:
Of whom God grant me of your grace
To be, that shall preserve this race.

Permit me voyage, Love, into your hands.